TO:

_____

WITH HOPE:

_____

Take What You Need

You Need

Soft Words for Hard Days

Aundi Kolber

TYNDALE
REFRESH®

Think Well. Live Well. Be Well.

Visit Tyndale online at tyndale.com.

Visit Aundi at aundikolber.com.

Tyndale, Tyndale's quill logo, *Tyndale Refresh*, and the Tyndale Refresh logo are registered trademarks of Tyndale House Ministries. Tyndale Refresh is a nonfiction imprint of Tyndale House Publishers, Carol Stream, Illinois.

Take What You Need: Soft Words for Hard Days

Designed by Eva M. Winters

Published in association with Don Gates of the literary agency The Gates Group; www.the-gates-group.com.

For information about special discounts for bulk purchases, please contact Tyndale House Publishers at csresponse@tyndale.com, or call 1-855-277-9400.

ISBN 979-8-4005-0347-4

Printed in China

31	30	29	28	27	26	25
7	6	5	4	3	2	1

—

For you, my dear reader—

may you come to know that your needs matter.

—

Contents

———

Introduction

—

READER, I AM DELIGHTED YOU'RE HERE. I pray that the pages ahead will serve as a soft spot to land and perhaps even a place to gather courage for the hard, beautiful work of being human.

Maybe you wonder what I mean by *take what you need*. As someone who navigated a traumatic childhood by becoming hyperattuned to what others wanted from me, I once feared making a decision that would displease someone else. This was certainly not the only way I adapted to the trauma I experienced, but I often depended on this strategy to protect me. I wanted to keep the peace at all costs, so instead of *taking what I needed*, I took what I perceived others thought was *okay* for me to need.

"Do you need help?" "Do you want to stay or go?" "Which restaurant sounds best?" Simple questions like these would fill me with anxiety and then a sinking feeling as I set aside my own preferences in favor of what I thought I *must* say. I unconsciously transferred the terror I felt toward my father to almost everyone else, following the template he'd given me about having needs and a voice. I learned to bypass my body, mind, and spirit very early as a strategy to survive. The shame I carried for even having needs was profound.

In my work as both a therapist and trauma survivor, I've learned how incredibly common it is for us to internalize the belief that we don't have a choice or voice in our own experience. These misperceptions frequently arise in the aftermath of actually having bits of agency ripped away. This is often the cost of unresolved trauma: that even after the event ends, our bodies still carry the imprint of the pain like a thousand splinters never removed.

It's not only trauma survivors who silence their inner voice. All of us trying to survive in a world filled with pain and destruction sometimes do so as well. How often do we disconnect from our internal compass—the part of us that knows if we're thirsty, hungry, sad, or alone—just to navigate all that comes our way?

Yet I have found that it's possible to reclaim connection to our God-given bodies and needs; in fact, it's foundational to healing and repair. It's more than okay to receive what we need so that we may participate with God in tending the wounds underneath.

I now recognize how essential it is to learn to tune in to the still, small voice inside of us that supports us in discernment. This is where we listen for *God with us*. This is what helps us know how to love our neighbors with integrity and authenticity. And this is where we can attend to the embedded wisdom placed within us.

In my clients, my readers, my loved ones, and myself, I have witnessed this hope-giving truth: As we return agency, affirm dignity, and honor our ability to listen to our God-given needs, we tap into the softness and strength of healing. We create space for repair.

I've come to think of the work I do as both a therapist and author as a sort of hospitality—a way in which I can offer nourishment where there may be fear, pain, loss, or trauma. Many of us are starved for hope, care, attunement, and compassion. Many of us are hungry, but for more than just food. Through the years, I have witnessed and experienced this feeling of lack; I know how it aches to be in need in body, mind, or spirit. So what I can offer is what has been given to me in my own healing. Our God promises to set a table with good things for us (see Psalm 23:5-6), and my desire is to follow His example. I want others to know that not only can we partake of all the sustenance the Lord provides, but we can do so in the way and at the pace that will actually support us. I invite *you*, dear reader, to take what *you* need in the pages ahead.

When the day is long. When you are afraid. When you don't know what to say to someone you love. When you feel alone. When you're questioning everything. When you wonder if God is with you. When the bottom falls out. When you don't know what's next. When you do something courageous. When you don't know how to have hope. When you need to know you can try softer. When you're learning to show up for yourself.

Reader, may these love notes invite you to truly listen to your body, mind, and soul. I hope you will honor your pace, engage what's helpful . . . and take what you need, in the way that you need.

With deep hope,

Aundi

Take What You Need When . . .
Exhaustion Looms Large

—

Perhaps you, too, know what it is like to feel overextended, overburdened, and overwrought, desperately clinging to the idea that if you just push hard enough, if you just try a little harder, you'll be able to regain control, soothe your anxious mind, and achieve some measure of success.

Our world overvalues productivity and others' opinions, so we learn to ignore the messages our bodies are giving us.

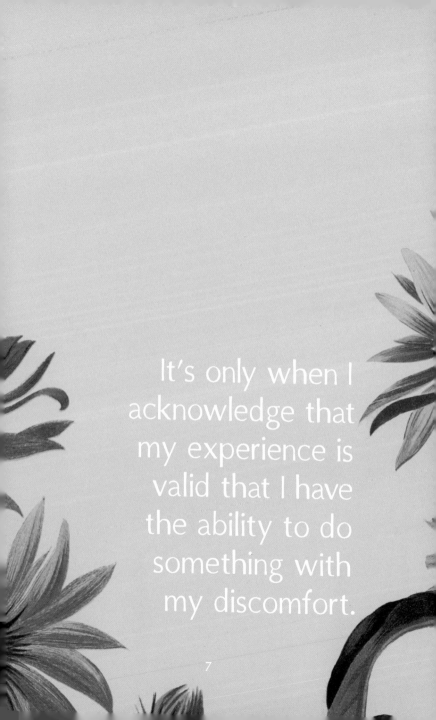

It's only when I acknowledge that my experience is valid that I have the ability to do something with my discomfort.

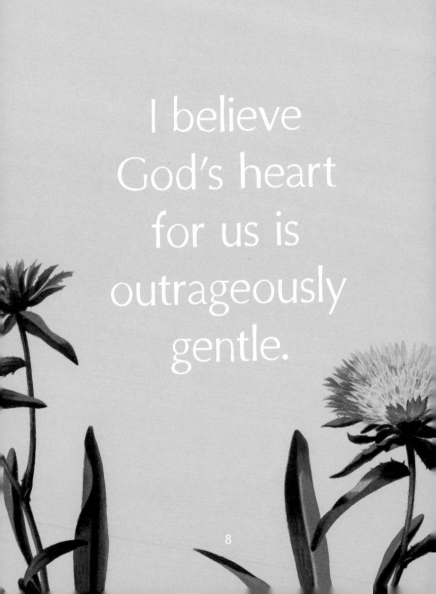

I believe
God's heart
for us is
outrageously
gentle.

You don't have to dismiss your pain here. You don't need to shrink it down or pretend living through it wasn't hard. You don't have to act like the shaming voices aren't still playing in your head, or like you're not still beating yourself up, or like the ways your needs were overlooked don't cut you daily. I'm not asking you to find the silver lining in your "hard." We know God is with us through it all, but that doesn't mean life hasn't cracked you open. It doesn't mean you haven't cried thousands of tears or spoken to yourself in ways you would never speak to another.

The wounds you have experienced are valid. Maybe no one has ever said that to you, so I hope you'll receive this now: What's happened in your life matters.

Psalm 56:8 says, "You keep track of all my sorrows. You have collected all my tears in your bottle. You have recorded each one in your book" (NLT). God is invested in the entire arc of our humanity.

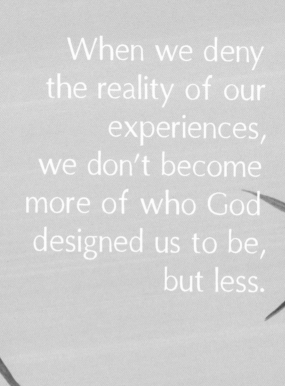

When we deny
the reality of our
experiences,
we don't become
more of who God
designed us to be,
but less.

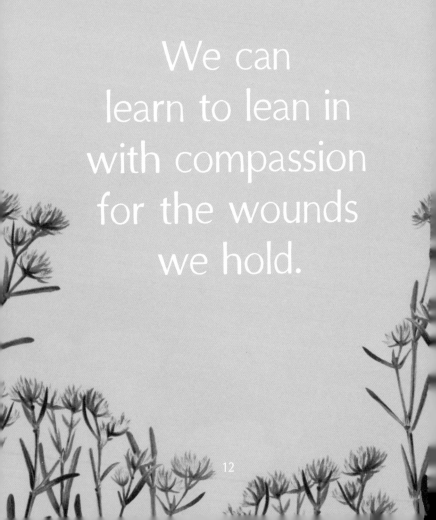

We can
learn to lean in
with compassion
for the wounds
we hold.

Dear one, I'm sorry you've experienced events that required you to survive rather than live. I'm sorry you've often felt alone and unseen. I'm sorry you've had to be so strong. And I'm sorry that you've never felt safe to be gentle with the parts of yourself that have needed tenderness so badly.

God's posture
toward any
fragmented, hurting
parts of yourself is
one of compassion.

May you
embrace this
good news.

Take What You Need When . . .
You're Weary of White-Knuckling

—

We've learned to white-knuckle our way through life to armor up against pain and difficulty; we believe minimizing our wounds is the only way we'll be loved. We try to appear successful, productive, or simply okay on the outside, even when we're not okay on the inside.

There are truly times
when the best, healthiest,
most productive thing
we can do is not to try
harder, but rather to try
softer: to compassionately
listen to our needs so we
can move through pain—
and ultimately life—with
more gentleness and
resilience.

Learning to try softer won't automatically erase the pain of shame, anxiety, or trauma. It won't make people love you differently. It will not take away the wounds already inflicted. It won't give you a different childhood. But it just might change *how* you go through pain.

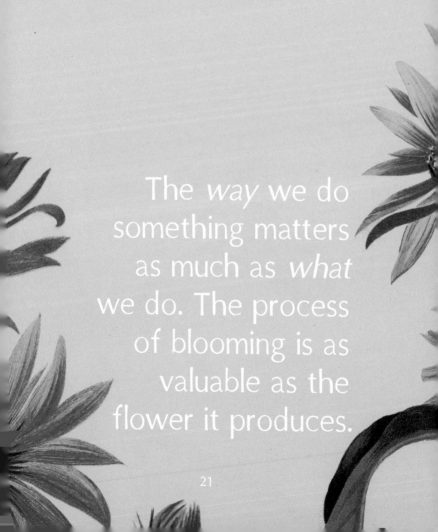

The *way* we do
something matters
as much as *what*
we do. The process
of blooming is as
valuable as the
flower it produces.

What would
happen if
you allowed yourself

to release
your grip on
this situation?

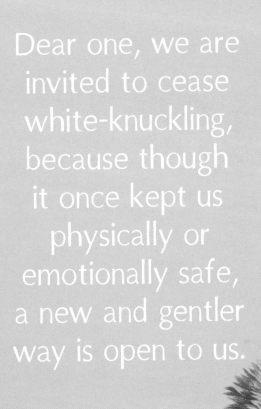

Dear one, we are
invited to cease
white-knuckling,
because though
it once kept us
physically or
emotionally safe,
a new and gentler
way is open to us.

Disappointing people *is* hard. And here's the thing: You will likely mess up as you practice setting limits. You will say yes when you mean no. You may take on too much at times. Perfection is not the point. It's about reestablishing your ability to honor your own voice, limits, and experience.

What if emotional health doesn't *always* look like being "the strong one"? What if sometimes it means stepping back and letting ourselves receive or grieve or feel? What if it's not just facing hard things—though that matters—but *also* knowing our limits? What if it's loving others, but *also letting* ourselves be loved?

We cannot "logic"
ourselves into safety
or out of trauma.

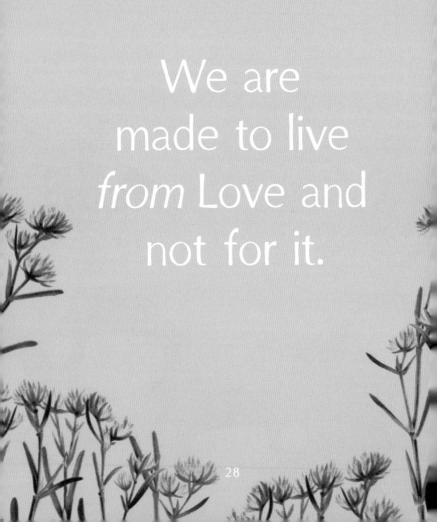

We are
made to live
from Love and
not for it.

Only love can truly lead us home;
only love can envision something
different from the patterns that
have kept us stuck.

Take What You Need When . . .
You Long to Know God
Is with You

The LORD himself goes before you and will be with you; he will never leave you nor forsake you. Do not be afraid; do not be discouraged.

DEUTERONOMY 31:8

Connection with God and others is the currency that allows each of us to experience coregulation.

Like the missing puzzle piece that fits snugly and completes the pictures of our lives, God Himself is our best resource—the safest, best attachment we could ever have.

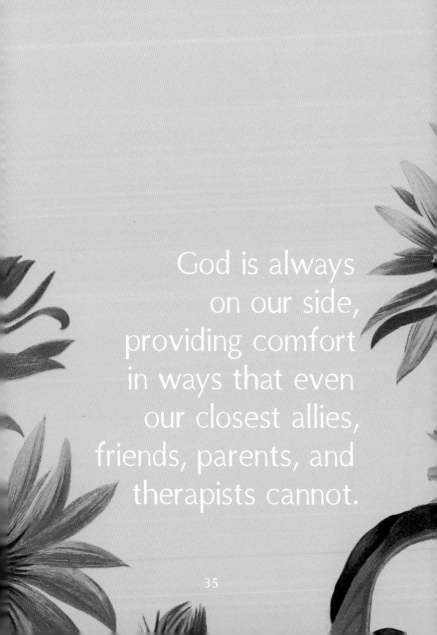

God is always
on our side,
providing comfort
in ways that even
our closest allies,
friends, parents, and
therapists cannot.

We are made
for relationship—
not just with
others but also
with ourselves.

Jesus' life on earth
says,
I choose to sacrifice
My body so you
can honor and
pay compassionate
attention to yours—
this is the length
to which I'll go
to love you.

Even if our
attachment styles
do not allow us to be
tender with ourselves
quite yet, we can still
experience God as
a safe landing place.
We can connect with
Him, knowing He
provides the security
we need to work
on our faults
without despair.

When we remember God's with-ness,
when we remember how God has
shown up for us, when we have
eyes to see the goodness around us
even through the smallest details of
nature, we can find glimmers of hope.
He is always making a way for us to
reconnect, to experience even the
smallest glimpses of safety.

God,
give me eyes to
see the ways
You're already
here. God,
You're with me.
You're with us.

If it feels like a supportive resource,
consider using this breath prayer:

Inhale: The LORD is a refuge
   for the oppressed,
Exhale: A stronghold in times
   of trouble.

PSALM 9:9

We can remember God's movement toward us before we even knew we needed Him. We can think of the verse "We love because he first loved us" (1 John 4:19). God created us with the intention to never leave us.

God is with us.
God does hold us,
even when we don't
know it. Even when
we can't hold on
to God, God holds
on to us.

May you
come to find
that the heartbeat
of God

is with you
and in you as
you embrace
this journey.

Take What You Need When . . . You Don't Know How to Get through Today

TRY-SOFTER LANGUAGE

If it feels like a helpful resource, take a few moments today to sit with one of the following questions:

- What is the gentlest thing I could do today?
- What words or affirmations remind me of my true self?
- I wonder if I could take this in smaller steps?
- What would help me stay in my window of tolerance?
- What kind of support do I need to make this happen?
- Whom could I reach out to if I'm feeling overwhelmed?
- How could I help my body feel safe right now?
- What part of myself needs support right now?
- What activity would be soothing for me when I'm feeling triggered?
- Is there a way I could move my body to help me feel more connected to myself?

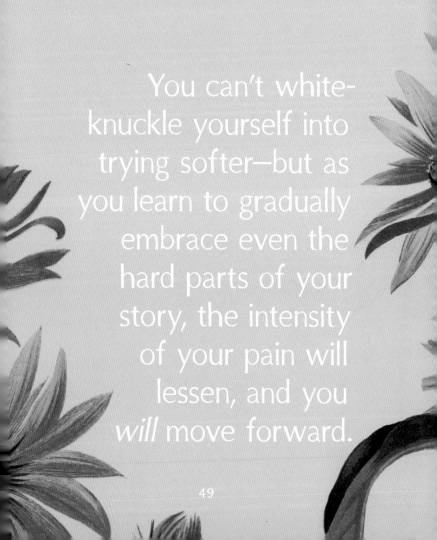

You can't white-knuckle yourself into trying softer—but as you learn to gradually embrace even the hard parts of your story, the intensity of your pain will lessen, and you *will* move forward.

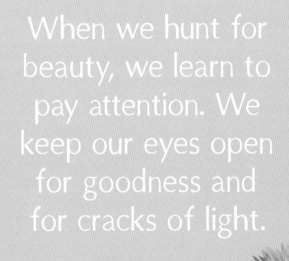

When we hunt for beauty, we learn to pay attention. We keep our eyes open for goodness and for cracks of light.

Be strong and courageous. Do not
be afraid; do not be discouraged,
for the LORD your God will be
with you wherever you go.

JOSHUA 1:9

Too often what begins as an adaptive strength in one situation becomes our default strength in all situations. It becomes our reflexive position as we move through life. It's as if our bodies carry the imprint of past pain in the next moment because we never fully metabolized that hurt in the first place. So we survive, yes, but we never thrive because we aren't experiencing the fullness God created us for.

What alternatives do we have? We begin by working to understand that it was never pain that made us strong in the first place. That we don't need to celebrate pain to cultivate strength.

Just as water can
change from a gas,
to a solid, to a rushing
river or a gently
flowing stream—so
too has God imbued
our bodies with this
ability to adapt;
this strength.

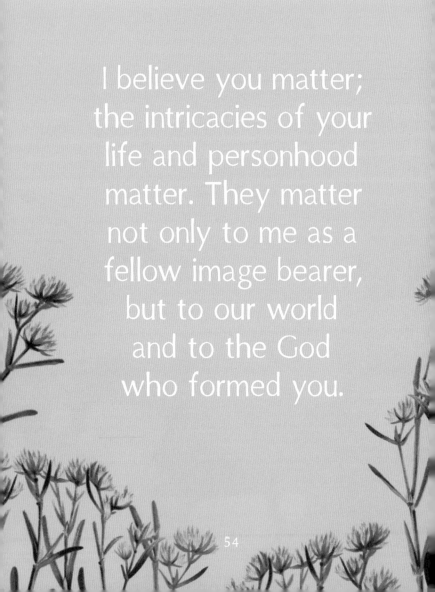

I believe you matter;
the intricacies of your
life and personhood
matter. They matter
not only to me as a
fellow image bearer,
but to our world
and to the God
who formed you.

Every time we feel the sun on our cheeks and the wind in our hair and the breath in our lungs; when we laugh at a joke or feel the embrace of people who love us, we are practicing the brave work of resurrection. In a world where there is much pain and destruction, seeing resurrection is no small thing.

Though we may be limited in what we can change, we can still leverage what *is* available now—even if that is only the knowledge that a past traumatic event was neither okay nor our fault and that it's now over.

Keep going.
But take
breaks.

Take What You Need When . . .
You Ache for Someone to Hold Space for You

—

We all need people who will spread their arms and create a space for us to be. We need them to see our lives and know us, whether we're being our messiest self or our best, most beautiful self. This essential need to be seen is part of how God put us together.

Feeling truly
understood
speaks to our
deepest needs
as humans.

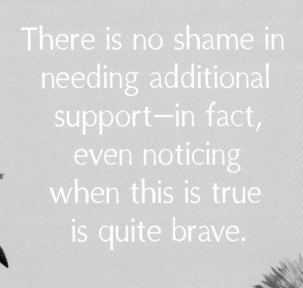

There is no shame in
needing additional
support—in fact,
even noticing
when this is true
is quite brave.

When the idea that "what doesn't kill you makes you stronger" plays out in real life, we see that it just doesn't hold up. What doesn't kill us can actually make us isolated, traumatized, and deeply harmed if we don't receive the support we need as we go through it.

The with-ness of God and the
with-ness of others are what create
the framework for what makes us
truly strong.

Love changes us in ways that fear and danger cannot.

When we feel
connected,
we have the
support to
be more fully
ourselves.

Connection is the remedy. Connection with myself. Connection with others. Connection with God. Connection is what creates enough safety for you and me to move along the flow of strength. It's this flexibility, not the rigidity of stress or trauma, that makes us strong. Connection is what expands into hope, courage, and life.

Moving toward those who are experiencing pain or working to alleviate suffering can help the people we're assisting, and it may also be good for us.

If we can truly
listen and love
our neighbor
as ourselves
for love's sake,
then we have
the opportunity
for beauty to
unfold.

Take What You Need When . . .
You're Learning to Show Up
for Yourself

—

Will this work be vulnerable? It will.

Will it cost you something? Indeed, it will.

But I promise you that this sacred work will be worth it—because *you* are worth it; every single one of us is worth it. I want you to know what it's like to be fully alive—not because you'll be perfect or because it will be easy, but because this is what we were made for: a living, breathing, moving, feeling, connected, embodied life. This—all of this—is your birthright.

This is the "try softer" life.

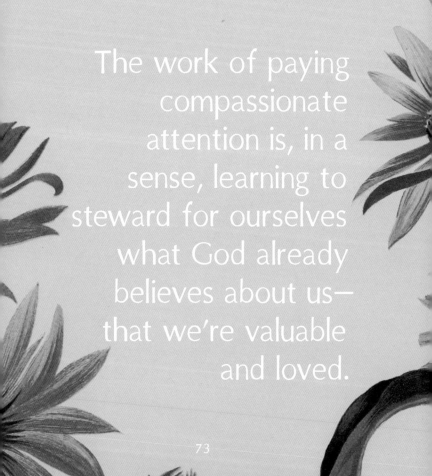

The work of paying
compassionate
attention is, in a
sense, learning to
steward for ourselves
what God already
believes about us—
that we're valuable
and loved.

Learning to embrace
our entire selves is
not just a spiritual or
mental endeavor—

it is also
an incarnational
one. We must
come home to
ourselves.

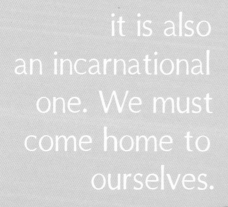

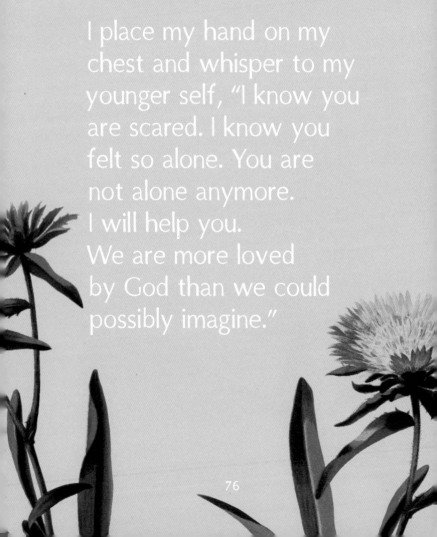

I place my hand on my chest and whisper to my younger self, "I know you are scared. I know you felt so alone. You are not alone anymore. I will help you. We are more loved by God than we could possibly imagine."

If it feels supportive, I invite you
to this prayer practice:

May I experience Christ's love.

May I experience Christ's peace.

May I experience Christ's presence.

May I experience Christ's compassion.

Think about everything you've survived
in your life. These moments are your
Ebenezers—"stones of help" that signify
what you have walked through and the
ways in which God has been with you
and loved you every step of the way.
And even though you continue to grow
and change, dear one, those stones are
yours to keep, reminders of how far
you've come.

Our capacity to
be alive grows as
we learn to process
and move through
hard things.

My dear, you are a shiny, resilient gem who has learned to survive hard things. Now you are invited to thrive.

Not a moment of your attention and care devoted to this work is lost—even if the journey ahead is long. For each of those moments communicates to your body that you are worthy of compassion and care.

The LORD is my shepherd, I lack nothing.
    He makes me lie down in green pastures,
he leads me beside quiet waters,
    he refreshes my soul.
He guides me along the right paths
    for his name's sake.
Even though I walk
    through the darkest valley,
I will fear no evil,
    for you are with me;
your rod and your staff,
    they comfort me.

You prepare a table before me
    in the presence of my enemies.
You anoint my head with oil;
    my cup overflows.
Surely your goodness and love will follow me
    all the days of my life,
and I will dwell in the house of the LORD
    forever.

PSALM 23:1-6

We were made *with* and *for* compassionate attention.

Even now, the work you are doing to learn about your body and your responses is beginning to lay the foundation for safety.

Look at you
doing this hard,
beautiful work.
Look at you.
I'm so proud
of you.

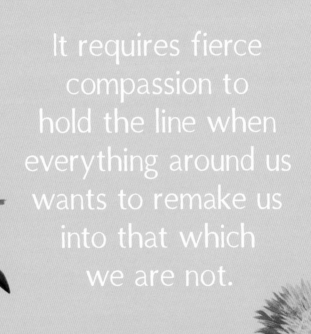

It requires fierce
compassion to
hold the line when
everything around us
wants to remake us
into that which
we are not.

Just as your softness is a gift,
so is your fire.

Take What You Need When
You've Forgotten Who You Are

During our hardest,
scariest times—
whether our bodies
feel stressed and
jumpy or sluggish
and slow—

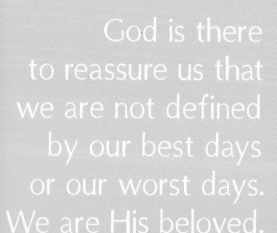

God is there
to reassure us that
we are not defined
by our best days
or our worst days.
We are His beloved.

The stories we weave and the meaning we make from them create templates for how we understand God, life, others, and ourselves. Regardless of the frameworks we carry, choosing to care for and nurture the whole history of who we are is connected to the way we were made to thrive.

"Even if the mountains walk away and the hills fall to pieces, my love won't walk away from you, my covenant commitment of peace won't fall apart." The GOD who has compassion on you says so.

ISAIAH 54:10, MSG

Emotions
add texture
to our lives.

What does a symphony sound like when we don't have the resonance in our bodies? What does a day out with our kids look like when we don't pause to recognize the beauty and experience gratitude? What does a broken heart mean if it does not cause pain? How do we learn that our words or actions are hurtful if we receive no reaction? What does love feel like with no emotional connection? Why should a baby continue to giggle if we don't crack a smile in return?

All the aching parts of myself are
beginning to speak up, to let me know
the extent of the pain they have carried
for so long—and instead of ignoring them,
acting like the pain isn't real, I get quiet.
I don't try to hustle my way out of
discomfort or shame myself for feeling
disconnected. Though it feels fragile and
new, I finally start to listen.

And there I find that my truest, wisest,
most compassionate self is finally ready
to speak up too. And boy, is she fierce.

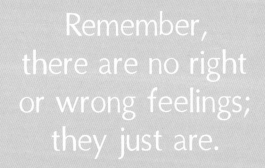

Remember,
there are no right
or wrong feelings;
they just are.

STRONG-LIKE-WATER LANGUAGE

As we begin to find a new way to be in the world, we often need new language to help honor our experiences. Feel free to take only what you need from the list:

- I can be soft and fierce.

- I can find people who help my body exhale.

- I can feel my emotions at the pace I am able.

- What once served me may no longer serve me.

- Surviving is good, but I am allowed to do more than exist.

- Discomfort is okay; harm is not.

- I can honor the pace of my body.

- Compassion will lead the way.

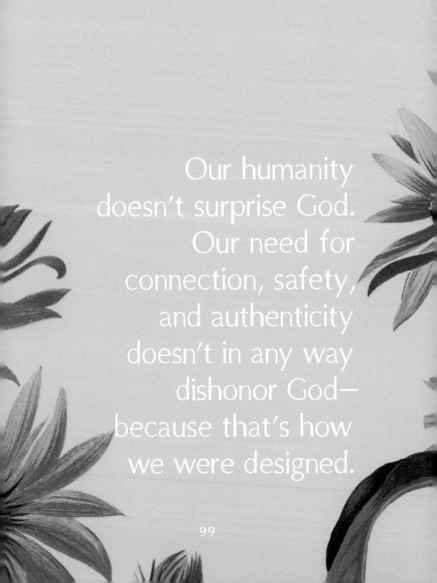

Our humanity
doesn't surprise God.
Our need for
connection, safety,
and authenticity
doesn't in any way
dishonor God—
because that's how
we were designed.

Take What You Need When . . .
You Don't Feel Worth It

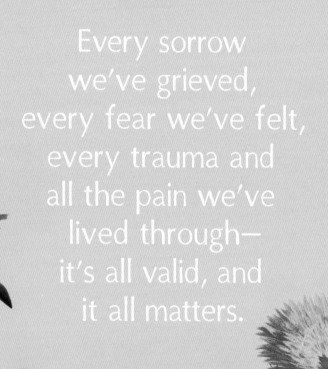

Every sorrow
we've grieved,
every fear we've felt,
every trauma and
all the pain we've
lived through—
it's all valid, and
it all matters.

You may have come to believe that emotional needs were a liability that led to shame, isolation, and neglect. You may have learned that the valid emotional support you needed to help you navigate the world just wasn't there. So now when a relationship becomes emotionally charged, you may feel a need to detach and isolate as a way to navigate the situation. My dear reader, this makes sense.

Little by little,
you'll begin to build a foundation
of internalized safety.

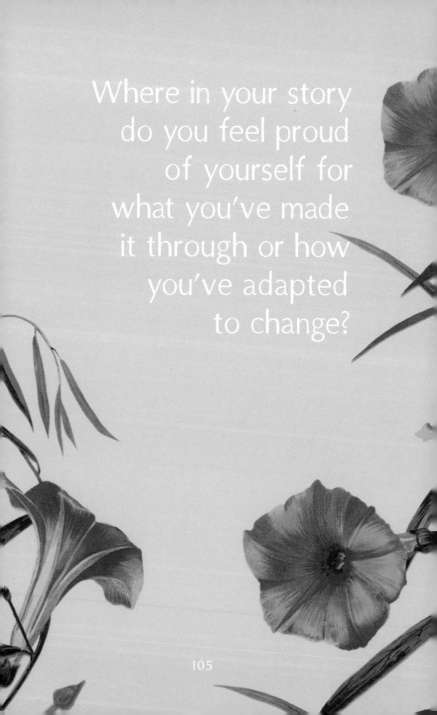

Where in your story
do you feel proud
of yourself for
what you've made
it through or how
you've adapted
to change?

Again and again He
comes for us;
He lovingly finds us.
He makes a way
where there was
no way.

If it feels like a supportive resource, consider whether any of these affirmations resonate:

If you feel afraid that the people you need won't show up: *I am loved no matter what—even when people mess up.*

If you tend to want to avoid connection when you are hurting: *It's okay to ask for help. It's brave to ask for help.*

If you feel disconnected from yourself, others, and the moment: *I am here, and it's okay to need connection.*

Our heavenly Father is kind, responsive, and steady, and He made us with the ability to internalize the reality that we aren't alone and are worthy of love. Though some parts of our minds may believe God is good, the work of trying softer is treating ourselves in the same way we believe He already sees us so that we can more deeply experience the reality of how we are loved.

I'm not saying that what we experience is *more* important than what someone else experiences, but it is *as* important as another's experience.

Emotions are like waves, meaning the experience of an emotion forms, builds toward its peak, and then decreases. Often if we can tolerate staying with the emotion for thirty seconds to a minute, we find that it will peak and then dissipate.

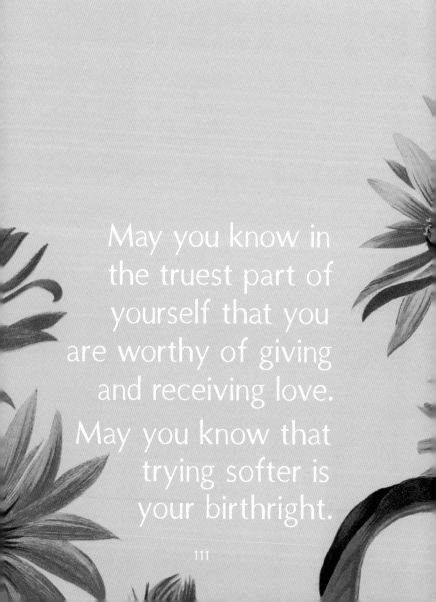

May you know in
the truest part of
yourself that you
are worthy of giving
and receiving love.
May you know that
trying softer is
your birthright.

I honor that the story you hold in your body is particular to you. What is not traumatizing or overwhelming for someone else might be *for you.*

I pray that as you walk, eat, sleep, cry, laugh, work, and tend to your life, you will sense that in each of these ordinary things you are already deeply known and loved.

When we don't have
the safety, support, or
resources to experience
the completeness
we need, it matters.

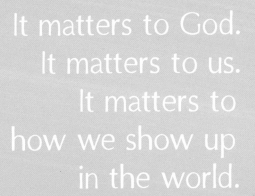

It matters to God.
It matters to us.
It matters to
how we show up
in the world.

Take What You Need When . . .
You Long for Permission to Rest

—

Are you tired? Worn out? Burned out on religion? Come to me. Get away with me and you'll recover your life. I'll show you how to take a real rest. Walk with me and work with me—watch how I do it. Learn the unforced rhythms of grace. I won't lay anything heavy or ill-fitting on you. Keep company with me and you'll learn to live freely and lightly.

MATTHEW 11:28-30, MSG

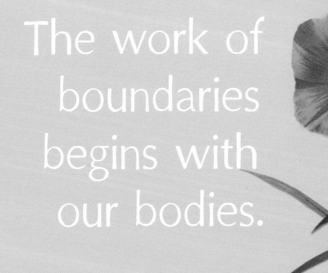

The work of
boundaries
begins with
our bodies.

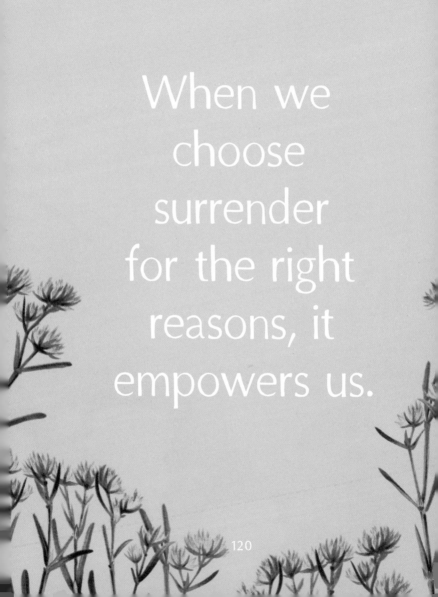

When we
choose
surrender
for the right
reasons, it
empowers us.

Both overwhelm and disconnect, in a sense, make us less ourselves. Yet the answer isn't to vilify our emotions or our humanity. Instead, we must learn to move through our emotions—to tolerate them but also learn to take breaks when needed.

Just as plants can't grow in soil
stripped of nutrients and nourishment,
neither can we.

The paradox of being
human is that we
need discomfort
to grow; but it must
occur at a pace and in
a way that our bodies
can tolerate.

We always want to honor the pace of our bodies, remembering that as trust is built, the internal relationship will strengthen and over time will be open to more connection.

Every time we
help our body
feel safe, we
are practicing
hope and
resurrection.

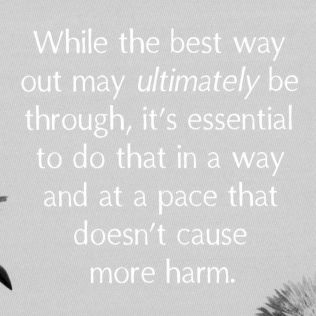

While the best way out may *ultimately* be through, it's essential to do that in a way and at a pace that doesn't cause more harm.

Deep work requires deep rest.

Take What You Need When . . .
Healing Feels Far Off

Learning to try softer is not a onetime
event but a way we learn to
be with ourselves.

It takes as long as it takes. It's okay to be unfinished. It's absolutely normal to be imperfect. It doesn't mean you're doing anything wrong.

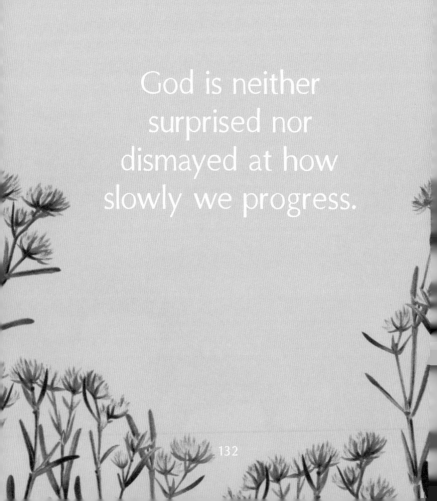

God is neither
surprised nor
dismayed at how
slowly we progress.

I do not want you to white-knuckle through your story; that's not what we're here for. Instead, think of our work in a circular way: We'll begin here, we'll move forward, and sometimes we'll come back to a place of examining our stories—not because we'll be stuck, but because this is all part of the process of healing.

If we can listen to and respond to our bodies' needs, whether that means releasing energy by getting outside or staying connected to ourselves through conscious breathing, our window of tolerance will begin to grow, and true healing can occur. It is slow work, but friend, nothing could be more worth it.

I hope you will not
allow yourself to be
satisfied until you
have truly tasted and
seen the goodness
available to you,
even if it is only
in spurts; even if
it feels fleeting.

And when you are weary, may you never—no, never—lose heart. May you know in an experiential, personal, and transformational way that the One who has called you is faithful.

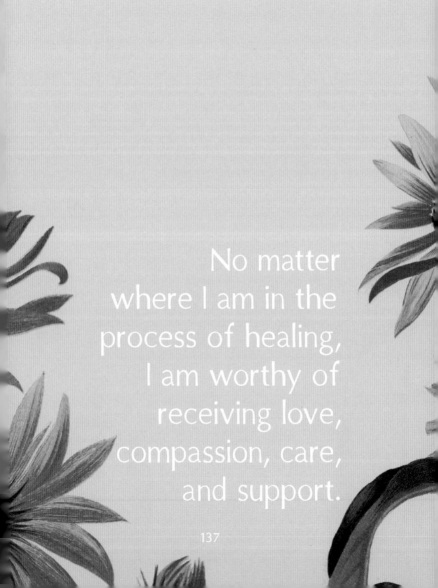

No matter
where I am in the
process of healing,
I am worthy of
receiving love,
compassion, care,
and support.

Trauma is not
(and never was) a gift.
But our bodies' ability
to adapt so that
we can survive?
That's the gift;
that's grace.
And it gives every
one of us a reason
to hope.

Occasionally we will find ourselves leaving our window of tolerance, even about a situation we thought we'd healed from. We may find ourselves turning back to a coping skill that isn't currently helpful (though perhaps, at some point, it may have helped us survive difficulty). Or we may say yes even when we meant to say no. We may discover that we feel disconnected and fragmented, even though we're doing all the "right" things.

Most of us love the idea of an open heart, of softness. But in reality, it's hard to hold on to that in a world that often permits—and sometimes even celebrates—brutality, violence, and harm. Often, we want to "guard the affections of [our] heart" (Proverbs 4:23, TPT) but we don't always know how. Sometimes we will miss the mark. We will have to reimagine more than once. There is compassion and grace available to us as we flex and bend, ebb and flow in our humanity. This will be our continual work: to participate with God in creating a new way; of co-creating a life that reflects the beauty of "on earth as it is in heaven."

We are not static beings who are planted in one way and place for all time. Instead, we have the God-given capacity to change, grow, and heal; we can return.

Take What You Need When . . .
You Don't Know What's Next

We have a Creator
who gives us what
we need to make
it through, to live
another day.

As the book of James tells us, "Every good and perfect gift is from above" (1:17). I believe that the desire of our bodies to survive is a gift.

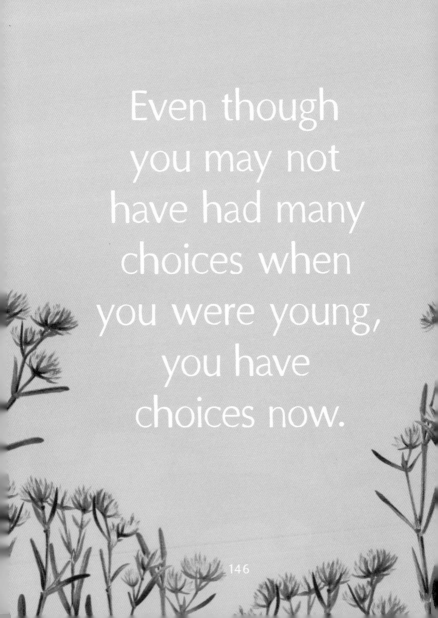

Even though
you may not
have had many
choices when
you were young,
you have
choices now.

Hold on to the truth as you are in the gray spaces of your life: You can and should find the goodness and glimmers of light along the way.

WAYS YOUR BODY COULD BE SPEAKING TO YOU

- Changes in temperature
- Sensations like tingling or heat
- Urges to move or flee
- Increase in heart rate
- Unexplained anxiety
- Unexplained heaviness
- Sudden alertness
- Feeling trapped or stuck

There isn't
one right way
to respond to
everything.

God is a keeper and curator of our stories. And every single part of those stories matters.

The LORD
longs to
be gracious
to you.

ISAIAH 30:18

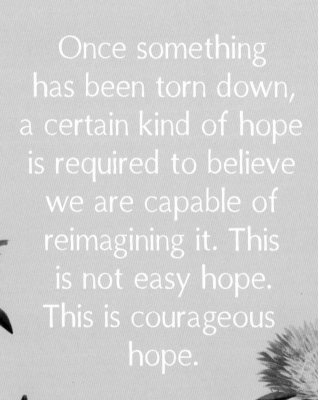

Once something
has been torn down,
a certain kind of hope
is required to believe
we are capable of
reimagining it. This
is not easy hope.
This is courageous
hope.

There is a mystery and cycle embedded
in the ebb and flow of life. For some
reason, loss and lament often create
fertile ground for tiny shoots of
new life.

Take What You Need When . . .
Everything Feels like Too Much

Many of us learned early on that setting limits is disrespectful and that being a "good Christian" means you have to give people what they want, no matter what.

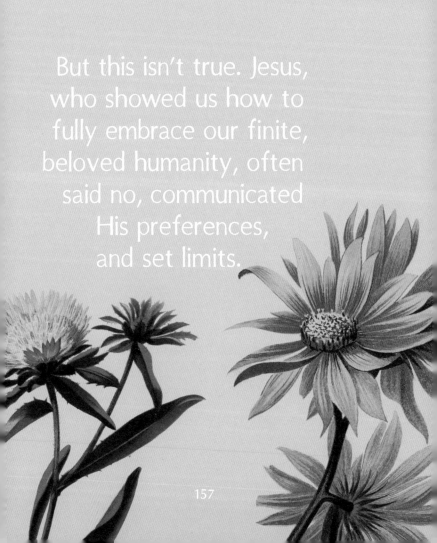

But this isn't true. Jesus,
who showed us how to
fully embrace our finite,
beloved humanity, often
said no, communicated
His preferences,
and set limits.

Learning how to be mindful of the sky,
a tiny crack in the sidewalk, or the
vibrant color of a flower can serve as
a bridge to learning how to tune in to
the frequency of our breath or the
sensations throughout our entire bodies.

You can put
down your heavy,
ill-fitting armor now
because you're
already so loved.

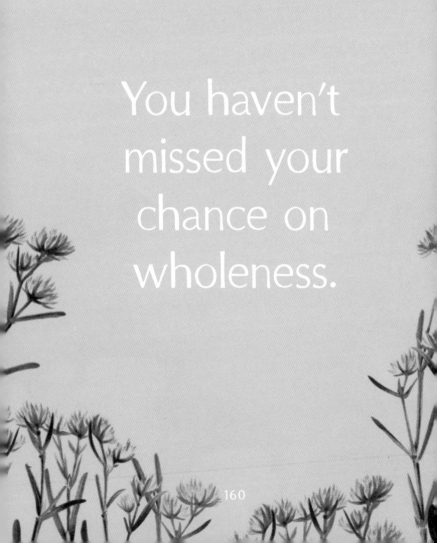

You haven't missed your chance on wholeness.

This feels hard, because it is hard.

RECONNECTING WITH YOURSELF THROUGH GROUNDING

Sometimes when we feel anxious or disconnected, grounding can help us find a way back to ourselves. If it feels like a supportive resource, consider engaging in this grounding practice:

Name five things you can see.

Name four things you can touch and touch them.

Name three things you can hear.

Name two things you can smell.

Name one thing you can taste.

We must learn
to fight to see—
and
hold tight to—
goodness.

Lament, in particular, is a way
of expressing our grief to God,
while knowing we are held.

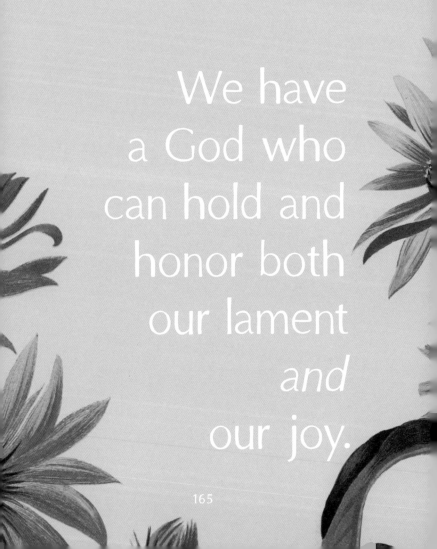

We have
a God who
can hold and
honor both
our lament
and
our joy.

Take What You Need When ...
You're on the Brink of
Something New

—

Love, hope, and safety
allow us to leverage, risk,
and face hard things from

a place of
resourcefulness that
is unavailable to us in
survival mode.

Little by little,
we build our
resilience—until
one day, we are
doing things we
never dreamed
possible.

Because our brains are shaped around
what we notice, it's important that we
become better and more effective
at listening—and responding—to what
our minds and bodies are telling us.

If we orient ourselves to the good, the true, the beautiful—to Love itself—we can begin to learn how to carry that around with us everywhere we go.

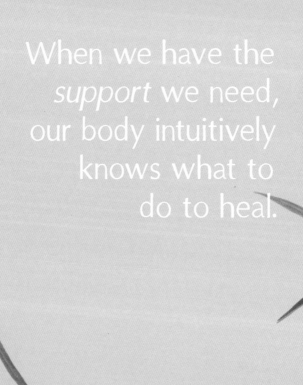

When we have the *support* we need, our body intuitively knows what to do to heal.

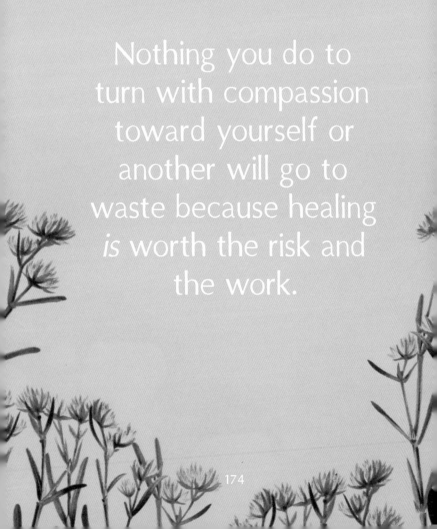

Nothing you do to turn with compassion toward yourself or another will go to waste because healing *is* worth the risk and the work.

May you find safety in places you
never dreamed and compassion in the
unlikeliest of connections. May every
moment of goodness you experience
begin to create a reservoir of hope in
your body from which you can draw
whenever you need. May each of your
senses be attuned to glimmers of beauty
and healing wherever they are available.
And when pain and difficulty come,
may you have the courage and tenacity
to honor them while also accessing
the compassionate resources that are
available to you now.

Take What You Need When . . .
You Could Use a Little More
Self-Compassion

—

Imagine actually experiencing tenderness toward who you are—not just tolerating or enduring your life, your family, your relationships, your body, and your career, but truly finding ways to love and honor them.

When we can
lovingly turn toward
our pain, expressed
in various ways
by our bodies,
we often begin
to find we have
choices we couldn't
see before.

CONSIDER PRACTICING MINDFULNESS IN YOUR EVERYDAY LIFE

- Put your hands under the faucet and notice the temperature of the water. Wash your hands and notice the varying sensations.

- Go outside and put your bare feet on the grass. Notice the textures and shades, etc. Notice the leaves on the trees. Count them; notice their shapes and their colors.

- Hug a loved one for five seconds. Notice your breathing, your heart rate, and any accompanying emotions.

- Read and meditate on the verse "Your beauty and love chase after me every day of my life" (Psalm 23:6, MSG).

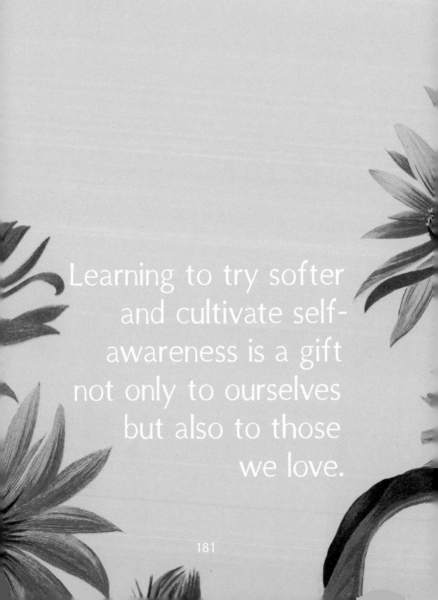

Learning to try softer
and cultivate self-
awareness is a gift
not only to ourselves
but also to those
we love.

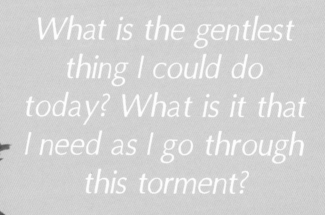

What is the gentlest thing I could do today? What is it that I need as I go through this torment?

Whether the trauma is big or little, people find great relief when they receive validation that their wounds need care.

I promise not to see my body as
something separate from me. As a
commodity. As something that must
earn approval to be loved. Just as I
am the beloved, so is my body. Just as
my psyche deserves compassionate
attention, so does my body.
My body is me.

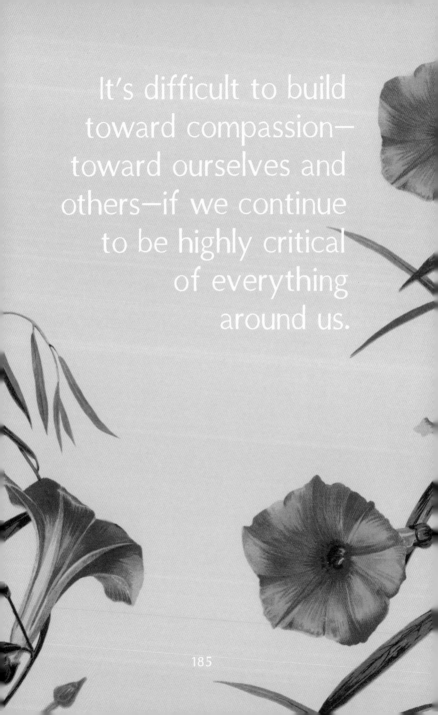

It's difficult to build toward compassion—toward ourselves and others—if we continue to be highly critical of everything around us.

Your grief, joy, anger, disgust, or fear does not define you, but it is a clue to what's going on inside you—and this is where the beauty happens. As we honor our experiences, we gain more freedom to move through our emotions rather than become stuck in them.

WAYS TO SPEAK TO YOUR BODY

If it feels like a supportive resource,
I invite you to use any of the affirmations
below:

- Thank you for supporting me.

- You can take up as much space as you
  need.

- Thank you for the feedback you are
  giving me.

- I want to listen to what you have to
  tell me.

- You are worthy of good things.

- You can untangle the pain that is wound
  inside of you.

- I will keep you safe.

Compassion is the ingredient that
allows us to truly access the love and
acceptance we already know are ours—
to integrate, open up, and create new
neural pathways between our wounded
parts and the loving, gentle ones.

God's posture
toward any
fragmented,
hurting parts
of yourself
is one of
compassion.

I invite you to take what you need from "A Prayer for Honoring":

God, here in this moment, empower me to honor everything that arises in my body, mind, and soul today; even if it means I have to return to it at another time.

Creator of all things, remind me that in honoring my experiences, You help me affirm dignity to the parts of myself that have at times felt stripped of it.

God, help me know that my desire for safety and connection is valid. In Your wisdom You designed me to need both.

But as I'm able, grant me the ability to open up to the possibilities of healing and newness while staying connected to the reality of Your love.

It's not
love your
neighbor *or*
love yourself.
It's love your
neighbor *as*
yourself.

Take What You Need When . . .
The Strength You Yearn for Is Soft

—

No matter how hard
we try, we can't hate
or shame ourselves
into change. Only
love can move us
toward true growth.

As you're able, take a moment to visualize your body in your mind's eye. Now, as though a laser were scanning your body for information, notice where you are experiencing any sensations, tingling, feelings of calm, or pleasant emotions. As you notice these, take a moment and simply place a hand on those parts of your body. Notice if any words or phrases pop up in your mind as you do this, such as "I'm capable" or "I'm strong." If you feel comfortable doing so, perhaps say to your body, "Thank you for giving me information. I am listening now." If this continues to feel pleasant, stay with this practice for thirty seconds to a minute, remembering you can stop whenever you want.

Even when we can't fully process an emotion in the moment, it is important for us to notice what we're feeling and give ourselves permission to name and honor what's there, knowing we can come back to it later.

The work of trying softer shouldn't feel like a bruising douse of pain from a fire hose. With beauty, it can feel like a homecoming.

I pray you feel rich
freedom to allow
yourself to listen—
maybe for the first
time—to the cries of
your mind, body,
heart, and soul.
And then,
as you're able, I pray
you will make space
for others to listen
to themselves too.

What if the truest strength is as expansive as the tide; the fierce and gentle elements dancing together as one? What if this strength has the flexibility to be both soft and bold; to both nourish and protect—because it is rooted in a foundation of love rather than fear?

What could life be like if you were strong like water?

This is not an indulgence. This is not a "nice thing to do if I can get to it," a "Sure, I'll stop and appreciate the flowers if I have the time."

This *is* the work,
dear ones.

As we learn to experience the full range of our emotions, we are *stronger and more resilient,* not weaker.

My fierceness
supported my
softness and my
softness supported
my fierceness.
I could be
expansive.

Take What You Need When ...
You Remember You're Loved
No Matter What

This is the Jesus I know and serve and give my life to; the One who holds the redemption story in one hand and the fragility of our human emotion in the other—and loves them both.

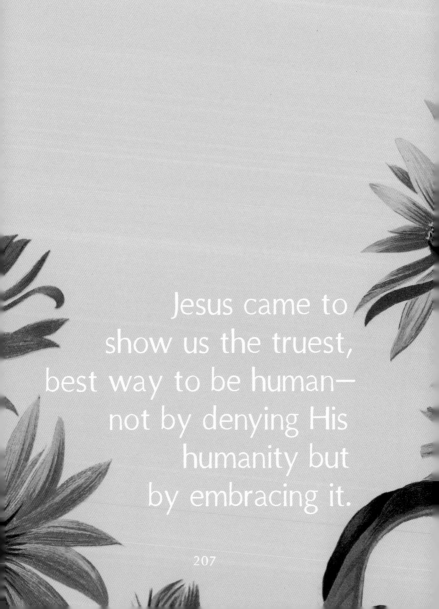

Jesus came to
show us the truest,
best way to be human—
not by denying His
humanity but
by embracing it.

What if this intense
dislike of ourselves
is keeping us
from embracing
the truest thing
about each of us—
our belovedness?

Trying softer isn't about *knowing* or *doing* the right thing; it's about being gentle with ourselves in the face of pain that is keeping us stuck.

Language struggles to convey the depth of goodness present in God's character—the way we are wrapped in His love and the way kindness has always been a part of who He is.

The kindness God
extends to us
is exactly as lovely
as we dare to
think.

Trying softer is not a destination but a way to journey through life. And it's in the trying, in the moving forward—sometimes slowly and haltingly—that we develop resilience.

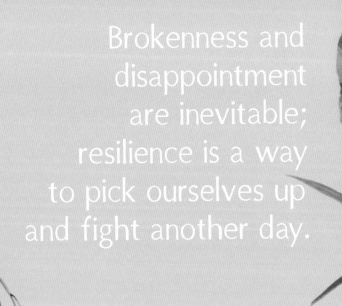

Brokenness and
disappointment
are inevitable;
resilience is a way
to pick ourselves up
and fight another day.

We get to
choose what
to cultivate
and what we
must learn
to forgive in
ourselves.

Even though we are limited and fragile,
our bodies can change and grow.
What a miracle.

My truest, most profound strength will never be found in denying the reality of my personhood or my story. Instead, the deepest strength has always, always been about welcoming them home.

May you be
met in the
fullness of
your humanity.

If You Want to
Go Deeper

———

Take What You Need When . . .
You Long to Know God Is with You

Take What You Need When . . .
You Don't Know How to Get through Today

Take What You Need When . . .
You Ache for Someone to Hold Space for You

Take What You Need When . . .
You're Learning to Show Up for Yourself

Take What You Need When . . .
You've Forgotten Who You Are

Take What You Need When . . .
Everything Feels like Too Much

Take What You Need When . . .
You're on the Brink of Something New

Take What You Need When . . .
You Could Use a Little More Self-Compassion

Take What You Need When . . .
The Strength You Yearn for Is Soft

Take What You Need When . . .
You Remember You're Loved No Matter What

About the Author

—

AUNDI KOLBER is a licensed professional counselor (LPC), speaker, and author of the groundbreaking *Try Softer* as well as *Try Softer Guided Journey*, *Strong like Water*, and *Strong like Water Guided Journey*. Aundi is the owner of Kolber Counseling, LLC, established in 2009. She has received additional training in her specialization of trauma- and body-centered therapies, including the highly researched and regarded eye movement desensitization and reprocessing (EMDR) therapy.

Aundi is passionate about the integration of faith and psychology, and is a sought-after expert in both faith and secular settings. She regularly speaks at local and national events, and she has appeared on *Good Morning America* as well as podcasts such as *The Lazy Genius* with Kendra Adachi, *Typology*, and *The Next Right Thing* with Emily P. Freeman. Aundi reaches an audience numbering in the tens of thousands via email and social media. You can find her at @aundikolber on Instagram or on her website at aundikolber.com.

As a survivor of trauma and a lifelong learner, Aundi brings hard-won knowledge around the work of change, the power of redemption, and the beauty of experiencing God *with* us in our pain. She is happily married to her best friend, Brendan, and is the proud mom of Matia and Jude.

Also by Aundi Kolber

Try Softer

Try Softer Guided Journey

Strong like Water

Strong like Water Guided Journey